MW01289069

HABITUDE WARRIORS

Principles to Master Your Time Habits

Developed by
SECRET HABITUDE WARRIORS COACH
ERIK 'MR AWESOME' SWANSON

TIME HABITUDE WARRIORS
BY ERIK SWANSON

This publication was printed in the
United States of America!

Published by:
Habitude Warrior International
Erik Swanson

in association with:
Elite Online Publishing
Sandy, UT 84070
www.EliteOnlinePublishing.com

ISBN-13: 978-1986637886
ISBN-10: 1986637883

Meet Erik Swanson

Erik Swanson has delivered over 5000 motivational presentations at conferences and meetings worldwide. As a leading award winning Professional Speaker, 5-Time Bestselling Author & Attitude Coach, Erik Swanson is in great demand! Speaking on average to more than 50,000 people per year, he is both versatile in his approach and super effective in a wide array of training topics. Erik's nickname is "**MR. AWESOME**" and you can find him sharing stages with his friends who are some of the most talented and most famous speakers of the world, such as Brian Tracy, Les Brown, Jack Canfield, Think & Grow Rich for Women's Sharon Lechter, Olympian Ruben Gonzalez, CEO Space Founder Berny Dohrmann, America's Business Coach Bill Walsh, the book *The Secret's* Loral Langemeier, Bob Proctor, and John Assaraf, and even the late, great Jim Rohn!
Erik Co-Authored the National Best-Seller '*Universal Wish*' with Greg Reid and the founder of *Make a Wish Foundation*, Frank Shankwitz!

Time Habitude Warriors

What others say about 'Mr. AWESOME'!

"Apply the HABITUDE WARRIOR Mindset and watch your habits and relationships change rapidly."
- Brian Tracy
- Bestselling Author/Speaker

"Invite Erik to speak to your group. You'll be glad you did!"
- Les Brown
- Author/Motivational Speaker

"Success is an art and science that can be taught and learned. Not only is Erik an excellent trainer, but his methods work in the real world with real people, right now! Get this book and apply what's inside and watch your sales soar!"
- John Assaraf
- New York Times Bestselling Author
"The Secret" and "The Answer"
and "Having it All"

"Mr. Swanson's techniques will not only increase your sales and time management skills, but also enhance your careers and lives!"
- Eric Lofholm
- International Sales Trainer & Coach

"Allow Erik's principles to change your life!"
- Greg Scott Reid
- Author/Speaker/Filmmaker

"In the journey of success you come across some amazing people who stand out of the crowd. Erik is one of those people! His books are jammed packed with nuggets to increase your income immediately! I highly recommend it. No wonder why we all call him *"Mr Awesome"!"*
- Loral Langemeier
- The Millionaire Maker & The Secret

"All we have is *time;* and *wishes* really do come true! Erik Swanson has done it again with his time-tested *Time Habitude Warriors*! You'll love it!"
- Frank Shankwitz
- Founder of Make A Wish Foundation

"Erik's principles to upgrade your income are priceless and include concepts every entrepreneur should initiate immediately!"
- Bill Walsh
- America's Small Business Expert

"Erik has done it again! Habits & Attitudes combined to enhance life efficiency and effectiveness …Absolutely!
Time Habitude Warriors is the book to read to leverage the gift of 24/7 to create and foster that **BIG** life we all want. **Awesome**!
- David Corbin
-Bestselling Author & Mentor to the Mentors

Time Habitude Warriors

Turn Your Next Meeting into an 'AWESOME' Event!

To book International Speaker and
5-Time Bestselling Author
ERIK 'MR AWESOME' SWANSON
Email us at
BookErik@SpeakerErik.com

TO DO LIST

NOT TO DO LIST

Time Habitude Warriors

"Your thoughts determine
your attitude.
Your attitude determines
your habits.
Your 'HABITUDES'
determine your future!"
-Erik Swanson.

Time Habitude Warriors

INTRODUCTION:

'To Do' or 'Not to Do'
That is the Question

To Do List or Not To Do List, that is the question! Let's face it, sometimes it's not only necessary to have an awesome 'to do' list, but we should also have a '**not** to do' list as well. As important as it is to make a comprehensive list of things to get done, it's equally or even of greater importance to list items you want to eliminate out of your day and life to become more productive. It seems so simple, yet so many individuals don't actually implement this idea. You will! This is a foundational principle of the Time Habitude Warrior. In this book, we give you 15 tips to implement on your 'To Do List' and 15 tips to implement on your 'Not To Do List' as well. Feel free to keep adding to these lists for your own personal journey. And please tell us how you do with your new found success traits. We love to hear your stories. In fact, simply go to www.HabitudeWarrior.com or email us at SuccessStories@HabitudeWarrior.com. We can't wait to hear from you.

1 DO THIS FIRST

First things first! You absolutely need to run out and get yourself a little binder or folder in which you're going to start using as a daily To Do and Not To Do list/calendar. You can use any type of system you would like to use, but make sure you use one! I like the little coil bound binders that have about 100 pages in them and you can stick in your pocket. That's what I use. Some people like to use their tablet or smartphone or even their laptop or computer. Whatever floats your boat; as long as you use something, anything! I call mine my "Time Binder."

WRITE IT DOWN: Start writing things down in your time binder for you to accomplish the next day. This is your 'To Do List.' It has been said and tested that there's more likely of a chance of you completing the items if they are actually written down and constantly in front of you. Each day when you complete each task or item, simply checkmark it off of your list. Notice I said 'checkmark' in a positive way, not to cross it out which doesn't give you that same positive celebration.

Time Habitude Warriors

"By failing to prepare,
you are preparing to fail."
- *Benjamin Franklin*

2 GET ORGANIZED

One of the best things you can do for your life is to get serious and organized. People tend to let things slide and things start piling up and before you know it you have a mess on your hands. Resolve to never be one of those people. In fact, studies tell us that clients prefer to work with individuals who present themselves well and are very organized.

***ORGANIZATION 101*:** The first thing you should do is a 'clean up' of your 'stuff' and do it now. Almost like 'Spring Cleaning' but don't wait until the Spring. You can do this in all areas of your life…your office, your car, your briefcase, your home, your closet, your computer or laptop, everywhere. Here's the rule to follow. Pick a location you will be doing a 'clean up' in and commit and resolve to do it. It should only take you 1 (one) day to complete, if that. Don't try and clean up multiple areas at once. You will only frustrate yourself. Pick one area and work that area. Here are the only 2 words you should think about: **'Stays' or 'Goes'!** Donate the items that you decide 'goes.'

"A goal without a plan
is just a wish."
- *Antoine de Saint-Exupéry*

3 BE AN OPPORTUNIST

Allow yourself to be an opportunist as much as possible. Opportunities are *always* there for the taking, but you have to be able to take full advantage of those awesome situations that arise. Just because opportunities show up in your life doesn't necessarily mean you are ready to seize those opportunities. I have always made it a point in my life to put myself in a position to seize those moments. Have you ever had a great opportunity show up and you said to yourself... "if I only were able to do that."? So, commit now to yourself to be that type of person who will take advantage of great opportunities that come your way. Take a chance! Life is about taking those calculated risks that pay off big rewards. When someone asks you to join them for something, say yes! Even though you're not familiar with it or knowledgeable about doing it... don't worry about it. Just go for it! People will start seeing that you are a 'go-getter' and somehow in this awesome universe, once people see that, they start sending more cool things your way and inviting you to do more and more in this awesome life! Do it!

"Never look back unless you are planning to go that way."
- Henry David Thoreau

4 BE PREPARED

When those opportunities arrive, you need to be prepared to accept those opportunities! Most people are not. I call this "PME" which stands for Positive Mental Environment. This is when you prepare in advance to mirror and accept good fortune in the future. For example, when I wanted to lose some weight, some of you know I lost about 24 lbs in a course of a three month period. For my "PME" I set out bottles of water all along the journey of my day so that it was a constant reminder for me to drink the water. You can use this theory and habitude in being prepared for other opportunities as well. Go ahead and make a list of areas you feel you could prepare more in advance for success and ultimately save time for yourself. Some other examples that I do may sound silly, but really save me time… such as, I have three different power cords for my laptops. I leave one in my office, one in my home, and one in my briefcase in the car. So, no matter what, I am covered. Another example is I leave a couple suits and shirts and ties in my car just in case I'm invited to speak to a group on the spot. Having two of the same thing is actually a great way to save time and be prepared.

"Give me six hours
to chop down a tree
and I will spend the first four
sharpening the axe."
- *Abraham Lincoln*

5 EVENT MANAGEMENT

Time management is notorious for being the #2 reason, statistically, why salespeople are not as successful as they would like to be. Can you guess what is the #1 reason that stands in a salesperson's way… it's **FEAR**! You know, the fear of failure; the fear of ridicule; the fear of trying the unknown; even the fear of success. Fear really is just a state of mind in which you can easily transform to assist you in harvesting great new habits! But, let's get back to 'time management.' Could you use an extra 2 or 3 hours per day? Do you sometimes feel you have too much month at the end of the money? Do you always feel like you need a vacation? Or worse, do you need a vacation from your vacation? Well, you're not alone. A ton of salespeople have this issue and it holds them back from the wild success that is simply waiting for them. The problem with most individuals is that they try to get everything done all at once, and they get in their own way. They want everything to be perfect and they keep focusing on becoming a perfectionist which in turn makes them stress out that they are not getting the important things done in their lives. That's the

"Habitude Warrior's" definition of 'Stress'... it's when you are not accomplishing the goals you have set out for yourself in the time perimeters you have allotted. It's tough, we know. I absolutely agree that this area is a killer in most sales careers. But, we are here to help! Here are some tips below to start implementing *immediately;* that's the key when it comes to time management.

Habit Tip 1: Act Immediately!

Don't delay! Use the Habitude principle "**Platinum Law of 48**" which simply says to act upon an idea and put your wheels in motion within a measure of 48! If it's a smaller idea or task act within *48 minutes*. If it's a business building idea then *48 hours* applies. And even if it's a personal goal or idea, act right away and do something, anything, towards the realization of that particular idea. Chances are if you do not implement the idea at hand within that time period then it will simply be wasted. This is where procrastination comes into play. The simple way to beat procrastination is to use these three simple, but powerful words and say to yourself: *DO IT NOW!*

Habit Tip 2: Time Block
(Event Management)

Use the time blocking theory in which you literally block out certain times of the day and workweek to complete certain tasks... such as blocking out 2 hours per day to answer emails. Personally, I block out 1 hour in the morning, and 1 hour in the afternoon. I also set up my email signature to let people know the times in which I return all email replies. This is super important to teach and train others how you would like to be treated. You need to let them know that they are not in control of your life and your time, but you are! Just like when we were little kids, we would have to let others know how we wanted to be treated in the playground. It's the same concept here. I use the same theory with my voicemail at work and cellular phone. Let people know when you plan to return all calls. They will respect you more for this technique. Finally, Event Management is simply a way for me to assure you that you can **not** manage time, but you can manage your events and the actions you take during each and every day. A good friend of mine, Terry Gogna, who resides in Toronto calls this 'PEM' standing for 'Priority Event Management'… which leads me to my next Habit Tip.

Habit Tip 3: Prioritize Your Day!

Start the night before. This is huge. Take at least 10 minutes at the end of your day to prioritize a list for you to accomplish the very next day. I can't tell you how important this tip is, yet, most people simply don't do it. It's very easy to do… and very easy not to do. You will be astonished at your success results once you implement this idea (Remember, use the Platinum Law of 48 and implement it over the next

2 days or 48 hours). Find a system and use it consistently. I use a spiral notepad for my daily prioritization. You can use your computer or tablet or smartphone instead if that works best for you. The point is to use one system and stick with it. Another point is to make sure this system you're using will be in front of you consistently each end of the day and each beginning of the day. This is called TOMA which stands for top of mind awareness. So, at the end, of each day you will write down 10 to 20 tasks or items you need to get accomplished the next day. Place the letter 'A' next to the tasks with the highest importance and Absolutely needs to get done. Place a 'B' next to the tasks that can take a Backseat 'til the afternoon. Place a 'C' next to the tasks that can be Continued over to the next day. Place a 'D' next to the tasks that can be Delegated to someone else (as in your assistant or outsource it). Place an 'E' next to the tasks that you can actually Eliminate out of your day completely and do not even need to be on your list. These last 2 are very liberating. It's a great feeling to know that you simply will never get everything done, nor do you need to. Practice 'Selective Procrastination' in which you procrastinate on items that simply don't hold a value in accomplishing. The way you can tell this is by asking yourself this golden question:

Does this task I'm about to work on have a direct positive impact in accomplishing one of my major definite goals? If it doesn't, then eliminate it altogether!

BONUS Habit Tip: "DOUBLE DOUBLE"

I wanted to share a bonus tip for you and let you know what I've been working on lately. It's called "Double Double" which to me is a Habitude Warrior commitment to myself in which I am committing to doubling my income from last year to this year; and at the same time, I will double the time off that I do it in. Pretty cool habit, don't you think? And what if I fail by 20%, 30% or even 50% … I'm still way ahead of the game! Challenge: Put this technique into action and commit in the next 48 minutes to do something, anything over the next 48 hours!!!

Habit Tip 2: 12 Business Cards Per Day

I always leave my home or hotel when traveling with at least 12 business cards in my wallet every single day. This is a habit now. Do it. It works. I commit myself to passing at least 12 business cards out per day. Sometimes I challenge myself and pass the 12 business cards out by noon. This means I have to meet 12 new business contacts before I can finish my actual day of work as a sales pro. This technique alone can change your career in a major way.

Habit Tip 3: 10 Social Media Contacts Per Day

Each day I make a point to connect with at least 10 contacts through any means of social media to grow my business. It only takes about 10 to 20 minutes per day to do this technique, but, wow, what a difference in results and awareness of what my company offers. Now, there are some rules to this technique. Don't, and I'll repeat, **don't** just send out the same 'copy and paste' email to 10 different contacts. You have to customize the email to them and introduce yourself quickly, but more importantly, ask them how you can assist them in growing **their** business. This is AWESOME and really gets amazing results in replies. The more you assist others to get what they want, then more the universe starts to deliver what you want. It's the most amazing thing!

"Motivation is what gets you started. Habit is what keeps you going."
-*Jim Rohn.*

Time Habitude Warriors

6 SET PRIORITIES

This is one of the best things you can do for your life and save so much time for yourself. Once you are clear on your priorities, the world of opportunities start opening up so many doors and windows that it will amaze you. We spoke about 'Event Prioritization' already. This is a little different. What I would like you to do is to set the big picture priorities. Here are the 5 major areas of goals and priorities in most people's lives: Career, Financial Income, Relationships and Family, Health and Fitness, and Spirituality. Most people have them subconsciously prioritized in that order as well. Take a moment and really give it some thought as to what your priorities are in each of these areas. Then, when working on that particular area, actually commit 1000% to concentrate in that particular area without letting other distractions get in your way. Ask yourself what it would cost you if you allowed yourself to get side-tracked in any one of these 5 major areas. Is it worth getting side-tracked?

"Create a definite plan for
carrying out your desire
and begin at once,
whether you are ready or not,
to put this plan into action."
- *Napoleon Hill*

Time Habitude Warriors

7 USE A POSITIVE ATTITUDE

You have a choice! It's completely up to you. Either way, occurrences are going to happen. It's totally up to you to choose the way you think throughout each and every day. Stop allowing other people to rent space in your mind. If you systematically remind yourself each day and in front of every challenge to ask yourself this question: "How would a positive leader think and feel in the midst of this experience?"... and then act and emulate this way. It sounds simple, doesn't it? Guess what, IT IS! It's that simple. They say 'common sense' isn't that common. Maintaining a positive attitude in my life has changed my life in so many ways. People now call me 'The Energy Guy' and 'Mr. Awesome!' I love that and wouldn't change it for the world. In fact, because I'm so positive, it literally rubs off on others throughout the day and makes the world spin just a bit nicer each day.

Be someone's **Awesomeness**!

But, remember, it starts within.

"A good plan,
violently executed now,
is better than a perfect plan
next week."
- *George Patton*

Time Habitude Warriors

USE POSITIVE AFFIRMATIONS

Try this and it will work for you just like it did for me. I actually hated affirmations. I would say to myself that those things just don't work. Guess what, I was affirming to myself that they wouldn't work. So, I decided to change my thought on it and start affirming things in the positive. It works!

Try these Time Management Affirmations

I am always early.
I am always on time.
Things always seem to work out.
Opportunities will absolutely open up.
I will complete this project on time and with ease.
I am going to order many of these Time Habitude
Warriors books for my whole team at my office and
all of my friends for gifts!

"He who every morning plans the transaction of the day and follows out that plan, carries a thread that will guide him through the maze of the most busy life. But where no plan is laid, where the disposal of time is surrendered merely to the chance of incidence, chaos will soon reign."
- *Victor Hugo*

9 TOUCH IT ONCE

A great Time Habitude to adopt in your everyday journey is the power of 'touching it once.' When something comes across your desk, vow to only touch it once. Most people spend way too much time on dealing with the same item that it becomes a huge & cumbersome task and starts to weigh you down for weeks. That's when the stress of that item or project starts to accumulate.

Touch it Once is a fantastic way to commit to yourself that you will handle that task right away and not let yourself procrastinate on it. Do not keep pushing it off until the next day. Take care of it right away and implement the ABC method we mentioned earlier. The awesome part of this technique is the amazing feeling you will experience when you make a great habit of it. It's such a fantastic feeling for your mental mindset to realize consciously and subconsciously that the task is complete and you can move on to bigger and better items. This frees up your day and it all adds up to more time on your hands.

"How did it get
so late so soon?"
- *Dr. Seuss*

Time Habitude Warriors

10 60 SECOND MORNING MIRROR

Take 60 seconds every morning when you get up and walk over to your mirror in the bathroom. Stare right into your own eyes and say these words:

I'm the best, I'm the best, I'm the best, I'm the best, I'm the best, I'm the best, I'm the best, I'm the best, I'm the best, I'm the best, I'm the best, I'm the best, I'm the best, I'm the best, I AM THE BEST!!!!

After about the tenth or twelfth time saying it, you actually start believing it. You need to pump yourself up in the morning (every morning) to make it an awesome day. I even write it on my mirror so I see it every morning. Who else better to pump yourself up than **YOU!**
YOU REALLY ARE THE BEST!
This technique saves so much time throughout the day.

Time Habitude Warriors

"Success is nothing more than a few simple disciplines, practiced every day."
-Jim Rohn.

11   HIRE AN ASSISTANT

You can't do it alone! I learned this the hard way for many years trying to take care of everything and wearing so many hats in my business. I should have opened up a 'hat' company. Do what **YOU** are great at and leave the rest to your assistants. This is such a time saver and life changer. There are so many people out there these days who would love some part-time work. Hire them. In fact, I pay a very nominal fee for my part-timers to work with parts of my organizations to do what they are best at. If you're an entrepreneur and just starting off you may feel like you can't afford it. Trust me, you can't afford *not* to get one. It truly frees up so much more time for you to concentrate on being the creative *you* each and every day.

Get an assistant so you can work on your assets!

Time Habitude Warriors

"Lost time is never
found again."
- Benjamin Franklin

12 DEVELOP A 'JV' SYSTEM

'JV' stands for "joint venture." It's imperative to growing your business. Remember, we can't do it all by ourselves. We need teams to help us. By developing a JV system, you free up a ton of your time while still bringing in the sales and revenue for your product or services. Having others promote and talk about you and your services gets the word around a lot quicker than you can ever do by yourself. And, the best part is that JV systems are set up on a commission basis once a sale is made. No need to pay until the sale or revenue is made. Our company has actually hired a JV Manager whose sole purpose is to search out joint venture opportunities and capitalize on them in a positive and profitable way. Having a joint venture in place simply duplicates you and your services and is a great way to same time.

"We can't do it all by ourselves, We all need a team to surround ourselves in our growth and success"
- Erik "Mr. Awesome" Swanson -

"If time were to take
on human form,
would she be your taskmaster
or freedom fighter?"
- *Richie Norton*

Time Habitude Warriors

13 SOCIAL MEDIA TIME

Let's face it, social media is here to stay and is what I call 'The New Normal.' And let's also face it, I think the internet is going to stick around as well. So, you have 2 choices: Either constantly complain OR confidently conquer! I choose to conquer. One of the best Time Habitude Warriors techniques I've developed for my business is to commit to introducing myself to at least 10 new social media contacts per day. But, you must do it in a natural and organic way... meaning write a nice quick personal note to these 10 new contacts per day. Get to know them. Find out how you can help them. Zig Ziglar used to tell us that the more you help others get what they want, the more you end up getting what you want. Join as many like-minded social media groups you can find that will assist you in aligning yourself with the right type of contacts.

"You gain strength, courage, and confidence every time you look fear in the face."
- Eleanor Roosevelt -

"The time you enjoy wasting
is definitely not wasted
time at all!"
- *Speaker Erik Swanson*

Time Habitude Warriors

14 JOIN A MASTERMIND GROUP

Benjamin Franklin, Napoleon Hill, Donald Trump, Brian Tracy, past United States Presidents and every highly successful person in the world all use the power of a master-mind group! These groups allow you to bring topics of super importance to the table with like-minded people, but from different vantage points and experiences. The awesome thing about joining a mastermind group is that 3 minds are better than 1... in fact, even 8 minds are better than 1, and so on. Search for one in your area. I also suggest starting your own group as well. This gives you more control to steer it in the direction and focus you intend. Allow the mastermind group be a nucleus of information and lessons from other's experiences. Remember to search out a group that is filled with individuals who are doing better than you in those areas you are trying to focus in on. This is how you grow. For more information just call our office or drop us an email at:
info@HabitudeWarrior.com

"The essence of self-discipline
is to do the important thing
rather than the urgent thing."
- *Barry Werner*

15 BECOME AN AUTHOR

Becoming an Author is one of the most vital coaching tips I can offer to my coaching clients. It opens so many doors! The problem is that most people seem to keep their 'book' inside of them forever. Dr. Wayne Dyer says people die with their song still inside of them. It's a fantastic feeling to be able to hand someone a copy of your book and present yourself as an 'authority' in that area. This Time Habitude Warriors book alone catapulted my business at least by 5 to 10 years! I use my books as actual 'business cards' to introduce myself to those who I'm looking to build business and alliances with. It's much better than simply giving a regular business card. The hardest part about becoming an Author to me was simply getting it done. I kept getting in my own way. I kept thinking it needs to be perfect. It doesn't. "Done" is better than "perfection." BECOME AN AUTHOR NOW! Become a published author today with the help of my publisher, Elite Online Publishing! Check it out at www.eliteonlinepublishing.com!!!

Time Habitude Warriors

"Learn how to be happy with what you have while you pursue all that you want."
-Jim Rohn.

Time Habitude Warriors

16 TIME WASTERS

DON'T DEAL WITH
TIME WASTERS!

There are so many 'Time Wasters' out there who will take up all of your time and leave you with nothing in return. Here are the 4 major categories of Time Wasters. See which ones you are wasting the most time on:

People who have no:

Need
Money
Urgency
Authority

"We are time's subjects,
and time bids be gone."
- *William Shakespeare*

17 BE A BIG LOSER

Be a Big Loser? YES, be a big loser! I learned this from my buddy Ruben Gonzalez who was once asked what he did for a living... He said he was a "luger." Which, right away they replied "don't call yourself that!" They didn't realize he was referring to the winter Olympic sport the Luge. So, it got me to thinking. One of my Habitudes is to train yourself to become a 'loser' in that you **lose** the bad attitude if you have one. You lose the ego if you bring that to the table one day. You lose that procrastination gland that so many of us have in our lives. What is something YOU CAN LOSE in your life that will open up so much more opportunities and doors of your dreams and goals? You know, it's not always a 'to do' list we need to have, but a 'NOT to do' list that truly makes a difference. Implement this Habitude and become a WINNER!

"Your attitude is too precious to hurt by
second-guessing yourself.
Protect your attitude because
it's the key to your future success"

- Ruben Gonzalez -

Time Habitude Warriors

"You can have it all.
Just not all at once."
- Oprah Winfrey

18 NEVER FILL UP TO FULL

This is one of those techniques that people call silly. But, I would much rather be silly and successful and drive away in my new convertible Porsche. So, here it is. You ready?

Never Fill Up To Full!

I never fill up my gas tank to full anymore. I started this technique a while ago to see if it would bring in more business for me and pay off. It did! So, here's the scoop. I only fill up my gas tank 1/2 full. This way, I'm at twice as many gas stations as you are. I get to strike up more conversations with the person on the other side of the pumps filling up their gas tank. Let me ask you a question... do you have a Butler? No? So, you fill up your own gas tank as well, right? Great, I want to meet you! It's a great way to prospect (Disclaimer: of course, BE CAREFUL of your surroundings always!). Just the other day I looked over and struck up a conversation about a person's Mercedes and we started comparing cars between our "S" Classes... It worked. He and I are meeting for a mastermind session in a few weeks. Give this a try.

"Time is the longest distance between two places."
- *Tennessee Williams*

19 FRIEND RENEWAL CONTRACTING

We all have friends. But, are they true friends? I teach this technique of Friend Renewal Contracting in order for you to free up more time in your life to actually meet the right people who should really be there. Let's face it, life and friends take up time. Are you spending that time wisely with those who are truly friends who are contributing to the betterment of you and others? It may seem harsh, but each year I suggest deciding who you would like to renew their 'friend card' with for the next year. Yup, that's right... I look at each of my relationships (friends and business) and determine whether it's worth renewing another year. Are they contributing to the positive enhancement of the relationship or are they acting like a reverse bank account in only taking withdrawals all the time instead of making valuable deposits into the relationship? You soon see who are time-wasters in your life. Here's a lesson: Stop chasing people who you are trying to give praise, money or awards. Honor yourself! You deserve it!

"You can't make up for lost time. You can only do better in the future."
- *Ashley Ormon*

20 DON'T ALLOW DISCOURAGEMENTS

It's inevitable; there are always going to be small setbacks and obstacles that may try to get in your way of success. Don't allow these small setbacks to get you down. It's completely up to you to have the willpower to identify the setback and simply decide to not allow it to affect you. You do have that power. Everyone has heard of mind over matter. Well, it's true that you can absolutely use your mind to control what *you allow to matter to you.* Make sense? Here's what I do: I remind myself that these small setbacks (notice that I keep saying 'small' setbacks, rather than allowing them to grow into big problems in my mind and worse in my life in reality) are merely there to give me the opportunity to grow and conquer over them. I also remind myself that it's a good thing that these setbacks were put in front of me because who better to handle them than me?! I can conquer over anything set in front of me and I vow to be positive and learn and grow from each encounter placed in front of me and see the opportunity each encounter holds.

Time Habitude Warriors

"Don't wish it was easier, wish you were better.
Don't wish for less problems, wish for more skills.
Don't wish for less challenge, wish for more wisdom."
-Jim Rohn.

21 DON'T GET OVERWHELMED

Don't get overwhelmed. Easy to say, huh? Well, this technique is an amazing way to keep your time management in line. People tend to focus on many things at once and get too overwhelmed, when in reality, simply focusing in on one task at hand and finishing it to completion saves you a tremendous amount of ramp-up time and completion time. It is said that a full 80% of your success will be derived by 20% of the items you focus in on. Even with that study, people tend to focus on the other 80% of non-productive items that lead to mediocrity. Remember, Jack of all trades is actually a detriment to managing your time effectively.

> "Until we can manage time,
> we can manage nothing else."
>
> *- Peter Drucker -*

"Time is what we want most,
but what we spend worst."
- *William Penn*

22 DON'T MAJOR IN MINOR

THINGS

If you take one thing from this book, this may be the one! A tremendous amount of people in society these days focus on all of the little items rather than looking at the big picture. The reason is that it feels good to accomplish all of those little items, yet it doesn't bring in the big rewards. It classifies you as 'busy', yet 'unproductive' in the ultimate goal of growth and success. This was a tough one for me to swallow... but until I realized the importance of hiring an assistant to manage these day-to-day items and tasks, I was simply wasting time. Nowadays, I actually have 12 assistants to carry out my operational tasks, while I focus in on the major tasks to grow my businesses. You would be surprised as to how many people out there in the world would love to work part-time as an assistant and grow with you into a full-time position and career. Guess what... that's where your business GROWS and takes off to new amazing heights!

"Yesterday is gone.
Tomorrow has not yet come.
We have only today.
Let us begin."
- *Mother Teresa*

23 DON'T GIVE YOUR LIFE TO

FACEBOOK

Don't get me wrong, Facebook is awesome! But, don't give your life to it. There are studies coming out that tell us an astonishing amount of time is devoted strictly to Facebook and has ruined people's businesses and even personal lives. I love Facebook and other social media outlets, but there's a time and place for it. Don't allow it to take over your day. I suggest you use our "Time Blocking Habitude" and literally schedule three 15 to 20 min sessions throughout the day to check your social media outlets. This will limit you to under an hour a day on average. I take it to another level where I hire 2 assistants whose sole purpose is to handle all of my social media connections and correspondence. It's called 'leveling up' in which you free up a ton of your time by entrusting others to take care of these other tasks. For your personal relationships, take this suggestion to heart: Limit only ONE session at home for 15/20 min. That's it! And then go spend some amazing quality time with your family! You're welcome!

"I must govern the clock,
not be governed by it."
- Golda Meir

24 DON'T LOOK FOR THE FREE

LUNCH

When I hear "free lunch," I typically run the other way! My time is super valuable and to enhance your own "Abundance Theory Habitude," I actually figure out how much my time is worth in dollar figures. Have you ever done this? It's easy to do, even if you're an entrepreneur. Check this out: All you have to do is ask yourself what your yearly income goal is for this year. For example, if it's $100,000, then you're hour is worth $50 dollars each hour. If your goal is $500,000, then you're hour is worth $250 an hour. $1M = $500 an hour. You get the point. Simply take 1/2 of your yearly income goal and drop the last 3 zeros. That's what your hour is actually worth if you average it throughout the year. So, ask yourself if you would spend that hourly rate to go spend time for a free lunch that someone is offering. The rule of thumb is that if someone is offering a free lunch, there's usually a catch. Habitude Tip: Simply ask them, to save time, what are they trying to accomplish so that you can prepare for the meeting.

"The best thing about the future is that it comes one day at a time."

- Abraham Lincoln

25 BUILD A 'NOT TO DO' LIST

Take 30 minutes right now and write down 30 items that you do throughout the day, week, month, that if you got rid of these items you would clear up so much more of your time. Let's face it, we tend to waste time. When I developed this list for myself, I started to see the value of eliminating these out of my life and started to see that I had a lot more time on my hands to focus in on my ultimate goals. Let's start right now and actually write down 5 major things you feel you're wasting your time on! Do it now!

1)_____

2)_____

3)_____

4)_____

5)_____

"When it lies in our power to do. It lies in our power not to do."
-Aristotle

26 DESIGNATE A 'NO CALL TIME'

Your time is valuable, yet have you ever met people who constantly think that your only existence in this world is to listen to them and their problems? Okay, so you know what I'm talking about then. I meet people who tell me they would like to just take a minute of my time, yet they try to take about 17 hours and you can't even send them an invoice fast enough before they are even finished talking. I'm kidding, sort of! I decided to designate a "no call time" for myself. I also instruct my team and assistants to honor this time where I simply do not accept phone calls during that time. It frees up my creative and productive time. Once you teach your clients, colleagues, and friends that you have these certain times that you designate, you will soon see them adhere to your 'call times' and success is much more attainable this way. Some of our clients actually mention these 'call times' on their outgoing voicemails. It's a great idea.

"Either you run the day or the day runs you."
- *Jim Rohn*

27 DON'T SELF PARK

This Time Habitude has to do with what we call the "Abundance Theory Habitude." What are you worth? A lot of people tend to try and save money by 'self parking' their vehicle, rather than investing in yourself and simply 'valet parking!' Let me explain a little further. I'm not offering this Habitude in a pompous way at all. I'm suggesting that there are many positive things that happen when you actually 'valet park.' First off, you feel terrific. It elevates your attitude. Secondly, you save time by walking to and from the parking lot. Third, you meet people while they are grabbing your vehicle. I have met so many people while standing there and striking up a conversation. Also, these people tend to be the ones you really want to meet and connect with.

Where else does this show up in your life? Could you apply this theory in different areas to enhance your attitude as well as save time, while also connecting with the right type of connections.

"The bad news is time flies.
The good news is
you're the pilot."
- *Michael Altshuler*

Time Habitude Warriors

DON'T SEND JOE TO DO MOE'S

JOB

I see so many people trying to send Joe to do Moe's job, and vice-versa. This tends to be a big waste of time. Find out what you and your team member's true attributes are and don't criss-cross them. Take a survey of each of your team members and find out what they are truly good and passionate about. Are they the creative type? Are they the 'get things done quick" type? Are they the "attention to detail" type? Are they the "customer service" oriented type? Find this out early and enhance their tasks surrounding their true abilities. This is where your team will grow and if you do this correctly you will soon have a well greased wheel of success at your fingertips. One of the biggest challenges of small business management is trying to mold someone into a position that doesn't meet or match their abilities. Better to hire someone right for the job, rather than try and mold them into that job and end up being counter-productive.

"The key is in not spending time, but in investing it."
- *Stephen R. Covey*

Time Habitude Warriors

29 DON'T FORGET TO DO

LESS

It's a proven study that 80% of your success will be attributed to 20% of the tasks that you spend your time on. This principle is so vital to realize and accept. Therefore, let's remember to focus in on the most important tasks that lead directly to your ultimate goal. There's a question I always ask myself every day:

Is what I'm doing now directly leading to the completion of my ultimate goal?

If it's not, then either eliminate that task or delegate it to one of your assistants or joint venture partners. Your time is too precious to waste. So, this principle of 'doing less' actually works in your favor. Don't over-promise people or worse, over-promise yourself. Focus on the vital few, rather than the irrelevant many.

"Once you have mastered time, you will understand how true it is that most people overestimate what they can accomplish in a year - and underestimate what they can achieve in a decade!
- *Anthony Robbins*

30 LEARN TO SAY 'NO'

This Time Habitude was a tough one at first for me to adopt, simply because I am a 'people-person' and love to help others. Yet, the power of the word "NO" really enhanced my time management skills and ultimately built more solid, sound and positive relationships in my businesses and even in my personal life. We all have the same exact time in the day. 24 hours. That's it. What you choose to do with it is vital. Realizing we simply can't do everything all of the time means you must choose where you will focus your time. I use what I call the "Cycle of Achievement" in which I have 5 major areas of my life that I focus time on. Here they are (not in any specific order) :

1) Financial Goals
2) Career Goals
3) Spiritual Goals
4) Family & Relationship Goals
5) Health Goals

Could you rate yourself in each of these areas on a scale of 1 to 10 and see how much time you're focusing in on each area.

Time Habitude Warriors

"Don't join an easy crowd; you won't grow. Go where the expectations and the demands to perform are high."
-Jim Rohn.

International Speaker &
5-Time Bestselling Author
Erik "Mr. Awesome" Swanson
SWANSON'S CREED

*** Would you like a copy of my Creed sent to you?
Email us your mailing address ***
info@HabitudeWarrior.com

SWANSON'S CREED !

I am the best
I am focused
I will succeed
I believe in myself
I have the will to win
I set high expectations
I visualize my perfect future
I don't let others bring me down
I surround myself with winners
I will learn and grow everyday !

About The Author

Erik Swanson has delivered over 5000 motivational presentations at conferences and meetings worldwide. As a leading award winning Professional Speaker, 5-Time Bestselling Author & Attitude Coach, Erik Swanson is in great demand! Speaking on average to more than 50,000 people per year, he is both versatile in his approach and super effective in a wide array of training topics. Erik's nickname is "**MR. AWESOME**" and you can find him sharing stages with his friends who are some of the most talented and most famous speakers of the world, such as Brian Tracy, Les Brown, Jack Canfield, Think & Grow Rich for Women's Sharon Lechter, Olympian Ruben Gonzalez, CEO Space Founder Berny Dohrmann, America's Business Coach Bill Walsh, the book *The Secret's* Loral Langemeier, Bob Proctor, and John Assaraf, and even the late, great Jim Rohn!

Erik Co-Authored the National Best-Seller '*Universal Wish*' with Greg Reid and the founder of *Make a Wish Foundation*, Frank Shankwitz!

Time Habitude Warriors

Turn Your Next Meeting into an 'AWESOME' Event!

To book International Speaker and
5-Time Bestselling Author
ERIK 'MR AWESOME' SWANSON
Email us at
BookErik@SpeakerErik.com

Read more books by Erik Swanson on Amazon

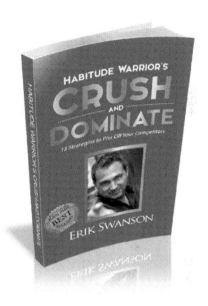

Habitude Warrior's Crush and Dominate:
13 Strategies to Piss Off Your Competitors

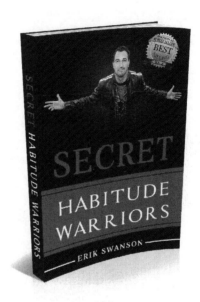

Secret Habitude Warriors

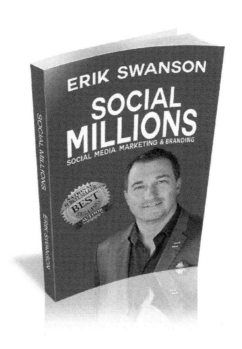

Social Millions:
Social Media, Marketing & Branding

Sales Habitude Warriors:
Sales Strategies that Lead to YES!

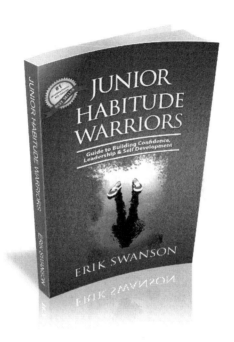

Junior Habitude Warriors:
Guide to Building Confidence, Leadership
& Personal Development

Write & Publish your book with
Elite Online Publishing

Contact them at
info@eliteonlinepublishing.com

93086162R00083

Made in the USA
Columbia, SC
08 April 2018